Contents

The United Kingdom 4

Land 6

Landmarks 8

Homes 10

Food 12

Clothes 14

Work 16

Transport 18

Language 20

School 22

Free time 24

Celebrations 26

The Arts 28

Factfile 30

Glossary 31

Index 32

The United Kingdom

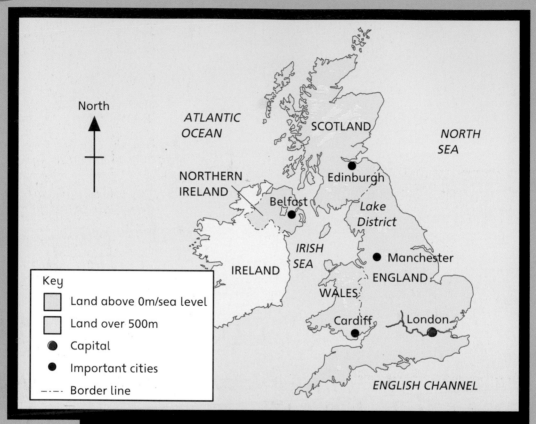

North

ATLANTIC
OCEAN

SCOTLAND

NORTH
SEA

NORTHERN
IRELAND

Edinburgh

Belfast

Lake
District

IRISH
SEA

Manchester

IRELAND

ENGLAND

WALES

Cardiff

London

ENGLISH CHANNEL

Key
- Land above 0m/sea level
- Land over 500m
- Capital
- Important cities
- Border line

Scotland, Wales, Northern Ireland and England
are in the United Kingdom.

The United Kingdom is made up of a large
island called Great Britain and hundreds of
little islands. Where do you think most of
these little islands are? The map will help you.

A Visit to the
UNITED KINGDOM

Rachael Bell

Heinemann
LIBRARY

First published in Great Britain by Heinemann Library,
Halley Court, Jordan Hill, Oxford OX2 8EJ,
a division of Reed Educational and Professional Publishing Ltd.

Heinemann is a registered trademark of Reed Educational & Professional Publishing Limited.

OXFORD MELBOURNE AUCKLAND
JOHANNESBURG BLANTYRE GABORONE
IBADAN PORTSMOUTH (NH) USA CHICAGO

Designed by AMR and Celia Floyd
Illustrations by Art Construction
Originated by Dot Gradations, Ltd
Printed and bound in Hong Kong/China

04 03 02 01 00
10 9 8 7 6 5 4 3 2 1

ISBN 0 431 08285 5
This book is also available in hardback (ISBN 0 431 08280 4).

British Library Cataloguing in Publication Data

Bell, Rachael, 1972–
   A visit to the United Kingdom. – (Take-off!)
   1. Great Britain – Geography – Juvenile literature 2. Great
   Britain – Social life and customs – 1945– – Juvenile
   literature
   I.Title II.The United Kingdom
   941'. 0859

Acknowledgements
The Publishers would like to thank the following for permission to reproduce photographs:
Ace Photo Agency: Geoff Smith p 8; Aviemore Photographic: p 27; Bubbles: Pauline Cutler p 14; Collections: Gena
Davies p 6, Roger Scruton p 12; Images Colour Library: pp 5, 7; J. Allan Cash Ltd: pp 11, 15, 17, 19, 21, 22, 23, 24, 26,
29; Link: Orde Eliason p 16, Sue Carpenter p 25; Shakespeare's Globe: p 28; The Anthony Blake Photo Library:
Gerrit Buntrock p 13; The Skyscan Photolibrary: p 10; Tony Stone Images: Penny Tweedie p 20; Trip: P Rauter p 9,
C Kapolka p 18.

Cover photograph reproduced with permission of Tony Stone Images/John Lamb

Our thanks to Sue Graves for her advice and expertise in the preparation of this book.

Every effort has been made to contact copyright holders of any material reproduced in this
book. Any omissions will be rectified in subsequent printings if notice is given to the Publisher

For more information about Heinemann Library books, or to order, please telephone +44(0)1865 888066, or send a
fax to +44(0)1865 314091. You can visit our website at www.heinemann.co.uk

Any words appearing in bold, **like this**, are explained in the Glossary.

This village is near the border of England and Wales.

Most people call the United Kingdom 'the UK', for short. There are four countries in the UK. These are England, Northern Ireland, Scotland and Wales. Look at the map on page 4 and find all these countries.

Land

There are many mountains and valleys in the north of the UK.

In Scotland and the north of England, there are mountains, deep valleys and lakes. In the south of England, there are gentle hills with wide rivers, where it is easier to grow **crops**.

Wales gets plenty of rain on the high land.

There is plenty of rain on the high land in
Wales. Rain makes grass grow well there. The
land in Wales is good for sheep farming. Sheep
farming is very important in Wales.

Landmarks

columns of rock

The Giant's Causeway is made of big columns of volcanic rock.

The Giant's Causeway in Northern Ireland is a strange **volcanic** rock by the sea. **Legend** says it was a giant's road that was built to step over the sea into Scotland. Can you see the big columns of volcanic rock?

The
Tower of
London

a
beefeater

Beefeaters protect the Tower of London.

London, the **capital** of the UK, has many famous buildings. The Tower of London was once a prison castle. Today, many **tourists** go to see its **keepers** and the **crown jewels**. The keepers of the Tower of London are called beefeaters.

Homes

Many houses in the UK were built over 100 years ago.

Most people in the UK live in towns or cities. Most people live in houses.

Nearly 7 million people live in London.

Many flats are built in city centres.

Some people live in blocks of flats. New ones are being built and some empty old buildings in city centres are being made into flats.

Food

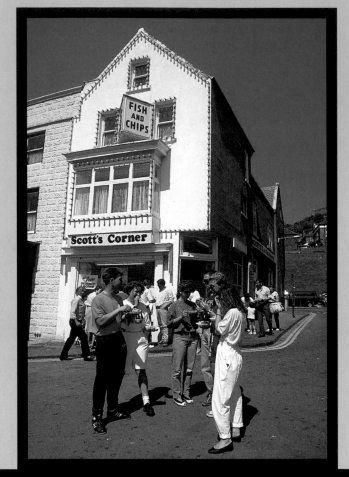

Every town in the UK has a fish and chip shop.

You will find a fish and chip shop in every town. Because the UK is an island, fishermen supply fresh fish throughout the year. Chips are a popular snack.

gravy

vegetables

roast beef

roast potatoes

Yorkshire puddings

A traditional Sunday lunch.

Different parts of the UK have their own special dishes. Yorkshire is famous for a special dish called Yorkshire pudding. Many families enjoy a **traditional** Sunday lunch of roast beef, Yorkshire pudding, roast potatoes, vegetables and **gravy**.

Clothes

Most young people wear trainers and sports clothes.

Many famous fashion designers come from the UK. Young people enjoy wearing clothes made by these top designers. Sports clothes and trainers are also very popular.

14

tartan kilt

Tartans can be different colours and patterns.

One of the **traditional** clothes in the UK is the tartan kilt. This is a checked wool skirt worn by Scottish men and women on special occasions.

Many people wear a tartan that is special to their family name.

Work

70% of people in the UK work in a service industry.

Seven out of ten people in the UK work in a service industry. This means that they work in transport, **education**, health and leisure, or money-related work.

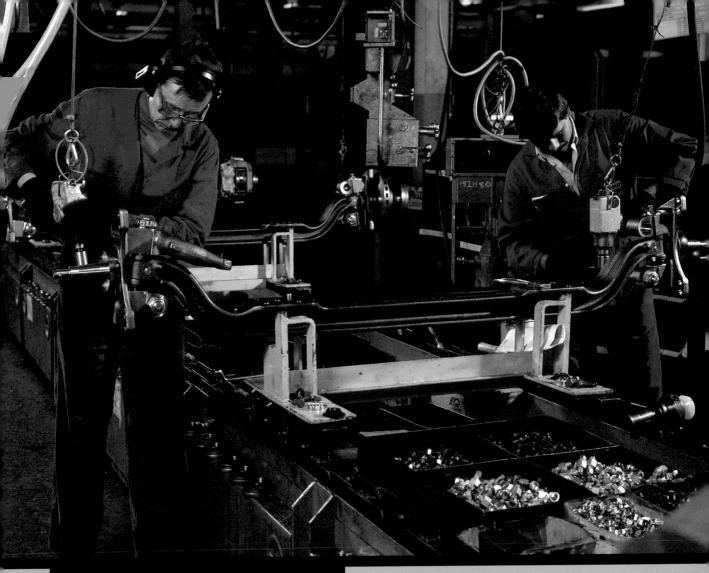

Some people work in industry.

Most other people work in industry. This means that they help to make or build things like cars, machinery and computers. Very few people work in farming in the UK.

Transport

Travelling on the Underground is a quick way to get around London.

The London Underground was opened 100 years ago and used **steam trains**! Now it uses electricity, and three million people travel on it every day.

Heavy traffic like this causes air pollution.

Most people travel to work by car and goods are transported by lorry. This means that the roads and motorways are very busy and there is a lot of air **pollution**.

Language

It can be hard to understand a different accent.

English is the most spoken language in the world. But in the UK, one person might not understand another because each area has a different **accent**. Which accent do you have?

This sign is written in Welsh and English.

In the UK about one million people speak Welsh and some people speak **Gaelic**. Some people speak other languages because their parents or grandparents came from other countries.

English is spoken in 45 countries around the world.

School

These young children are painting outside.

Children have to go to school from the age of 5 until they are 16. They study science, geography, history, English, music, maths, art and physical education.

Parents pay money for their children to go to this school.

Most schools are free and children from the local area go there. Some schools are not free and parents are charged money. Some children can even sleep at schools called boarding schools.

Free time

Many people wear their team's colours to matches.

Many famous sports have come from the UK, like football, tennis and cricket. Children play these both in and out of school. Many adults and children like to watch sport.

Over 21 million people watched football matches in 1998!

When you were younger did you ever have a donkey ride on the beach?

Many people enjoy being outdoors. Some go to the beach in summer. Others go walking or cycling in the mountains in the Lake District or Scotland. What do you like to do in summer?

Celebrations

The streets are brightly lit at Christmas time.

The biggest celebration of the whole year for Christians is Christmas. The streets are lit with Christmas lights. People buy presents for each other and eat special Christmas food. Which special days do you celebrate?

On Burns' Night, people say poems written by Robert Burns.

Another special celebration in Scotland is Burns' Night. Robert Burns was a famous Scottish poet. On Burns' Night, people wear tartan clothes and eat a special food called haggis.

The Arts

The Globe Theatre, London.

The UK is famous for its theatre. There are many theatres and theatre festivals to visit. Many people like to go to the theatre to see one of **Shakespeare's** plays.

A choir competes in the Eisteddfod festival.

The UK has many musicians and pop groups. In Wales the Eisteddfod festival is a big competition for people who sing, write poetry or play music.

Factfile

Name   The full name of the UK is the United Kingdom of Great Britain and Northern Ireland.

Capital   The **capital** city of the United Kingdom is London.

Language Most people speak English, but some also speak Welsh or **Gaelic**.

Population There are about 58 million people living in the United Kingdom.

Money   The English have the pound (£), which is divided into 100 pence. The Irish pound is called a punt. Scotland and Wales also have their own coins and bank notes.

Religion There are many Christians in the United Kingdom, as well as Muslims, Sikhs, Hindus, Jews and Buddhists.

Products The United Kingdom produces oil and gas, wheat and other foods, chemicals, cars and other transport machinery.

Words you can learn

These words are Welsh Gaelic.

diolch (DEE-olkh)	thank you
bore da (boh-re-DAR)	good morning
nos da (norse-dar)	good night
hwyl fawr (hooeel-vowr)	goodbye
ie (EE-eh)	yes
na (nar)	no

Glossary

accent	a different way of saying the same word
capital	the city where the government is based
crops	the plants that farmers grow
crown jewels	the crowns and special jewels worn by the Queen of Great Britain
education	anything to do with teaching children or adults
Gaelic	the ancient language of the people who first lived in Ireland, Wales, and Breton in France
gravy	meat juices that are made into a sauce
keepers	people who wear special clothes and protect a building
legend	a well-known, old story
pollution	dirt and poisons that fill the air, usually made by car and lorry engines
Shakespeare	a man who lived over 400 years ago. He wrote plays and poems that are still popular today
steam train	an old type of train that burned coal to make steam which made the engine work
tourists	people who travel to other places for holidays or to see the sights
traditional	the way things have been done or made for a long time
volcanic	a type of rock that has melted and is pushed out from beneath the Earth's surface

Index

Christmas   26

Gaelic   21, 30

Giant's Causeway   8

Great Britain   4, 30

Lake District   25

London   9, 18, 30

London Underground   18

mountains   6, 25

Northern Ireland   4, 5, 8, 30

rain   7

Scotland   5, 27, 30

Shakespeare   28

Tower of London   9

Wales   5, 29, 30